Hymns of Lamentation

J Renee Sterrett

BookLeaf Publishing

Presentation by *BookLeaf Publishing*

Web: www.bookleafpub.com

E-mail: info@bookleafpub.com

ISBN: 9789357211192

First edition 2022

DEDICATION

In loving memory of Benita L. Smith, your legacy will forever live through me.

To my dear mother who loved me with pure agape love, I can never repay you for the way that you mothered me unapologetically and with so much tenderness and grace.

To the love of my life C Cierra J Brown Hinton, your love is a salve and healing is what my poetry has always been made of.

To my students, past, present, and future, I am because you are.

ACKNOWLEDGEMENT

I extend love and gratitude to the Thompson 5 with special thanks to my best friend Lee, for keeping me alive long enough to get me to a place of healing. You continue to teach me that familial love goes beyond the bounds of blood.

Many thanks to A Rae, Eris, Bianca, NeoSouljah, Tom, Justice, Free, B Lynn, and Ko who taught me to believe in the natural evolution of my craft. Thank you for the encouragement, support, and challenge that allowed me to keep writing through all of the struggle and unbelief.

PREFACE

I used to joke that I was born on the altar and drank from scripture-infused bottles. Church has always been a part of my world. You can take the kid out of the church but you can't take the church out of the kid. Gospel is still music that resonates, I still move my arms to direct the choir, and I still hold the microphone as the scared kid hoping this solo wasn't dissected at the next family meal.

My relationship with God, church, and family is complicated. This collection is birthed from the intimacy of their trinity while processing all the things that helped me survive and almost killed me at the same time. To be Black Queer and Christian is a complicated web of learning and unlearning when you were raised in it from an elitist evangelical lens.

BAPTISM

Listen to the water
Let her melody
Lead you home

Take me to the water

Ancestors jump
To eternal fate
As they escape
The wiles of slavery
They leap toward destiny
Refusing to be controlled

Take me to the water

Thirsting souls run
Panting and begging
Immersed in living water
Restoring dehydrated spirits
From wells of holiness
So they never thirst again

Take me to the water

Waves overtaking bodies
Crashing in songs of praise

Liberation resonates
In fluid movements
Born beneath the surface
As angels trouble them

To be baptized

Sins washed clean
Scrubbed infirmities
Cause dead men to rise
Purified from wickedness
Submergence becomes
Wholeness in the making

In the name of Jesus

Walking on water
Calming raging seas
Unafraid and in control
Calling winds to peace
Storm clouds roll away
And we are safe

In the name of Jesus

Purity turned festivity
Made wine celebrating
Miraculous soul-stirring
Spiritually inebriated
Liturgical dancing
Reviving our souls

In the name of Jesus

Bodies washed in buckets
Salvation sprinkles faith
On clear consciousness
Sweeping over rivers
Springing abundance
Defeating our yearning

To be baptized

AMERICAN SON

Last night I became new
Versions of old
Black mothers birthing sons
Mourning in a world
Seeking their destruction

Their eloquent rage
Bubbled into bellowing
Outcries of travailings
And wails lodged in crevices
Tucked between my survival
And their suffering

Her sweat poured from
My brow baptizing babies born
Dying between feces and vomit
Excretions joining waste's company
In the pile of shit beneath me

I labored in her anguish
Weeping at my failure
To protect our sons from hawking
Neglecting to shield them
From spirits devouring their bodies
She did nothing as they laid down

And died right beside me

I breathed her faith
On ships of desolation
My survival her salvation
She foresees freedom long
Before it's coming drumming
The beat of ancestral footsteps
Sent to guide her in faith
I'd follow behind them

Last night I resurfaced
Heartache crying for generations
Of Mothers sons ripped
From our arms endangered
In murderous shadows
That stole our land
Their lives and mine

SEEDS OF ABRAHAM

He planted his insecurity
In her womb she birthed
Me traveling dark canals
Through fear restricted airways
Leaving me gasping
First moments of unworthiness
Manifested in a fight for survival

I leaped into her arms
His face rushed to claim me
Her genes lodged in the sanctity
Of her love swaddling me
Hidden from the demons
Transmitted through his deposit

His admiration rapidly morphed
Into furrowed brows of disappointment
Whips and welts of shame raised me
In remorse she bathed me in tears
Cleansed me from guilt's stain
In the stripes that refused to heal

He abandoned me I ran
Into the arms of many men
Who never loved me but stroked

The endorphins attached to my desire
Indulgence planted his immorality
My womb refused his blessing

She begged me to birth
Redemption I never could
He berated me into ideals
Where I found no solace
I was the source of her sorrow
He blamed me for his guilt
I remained empty no harvest
Fruit don't yield from seeds
Planted in desolation

INTERIOR DESIGN

I contorted
My extremities
Into decor

For image

For acceptance

For the culture

Gratification as immediate
Positive response
Hanging from the walls
Of my otherwise
Humble abode

Validation bathing
My insecurities in Sunday
Morning consecration
Bubbles born into salve
Applied to my brokenness

Tender hands
Kill me softly
Gripping my voice

In the swelling
Silence

I cannot dissent
Or consent
If I remain voiceless

I step out
On faith to wrap
My melting vulnerability
In bundled reassurance

Lay me down to sleep
Where dreams become
Nighmare's realities
Or I rest in peace

It's hard to know

RECYCLABLE

I carry the burden of my mother's perceived
privilege
On my skin's emphatic rejection
Bucking systems where I remain unwanted

Deficiency forced humility subtle
Disapproval negates desirability
Speaking truth in case I'd somehow forgotten

I carry my father's degradation in my bones
Harvesting acceptance planting my love
Where it refuses to grow a new high

Disposable traces erase justified infractions
Thrown me away not good enough
In the first place sabotage the winning trick

I carry my brother's dissipating innocence in my
head
Cynicism explodes into skeptical bits of distrust
I wasn't protected like I was supposed to

Precarious behavior hazardous refuted
arguments

Substantiated invincibility reduced to human
Suffering maybe love comes when it’s finished

I haul my family lineage on broadened shoulders
Capitalism’s workhorse indentured servitude
For change efforts go unpaid afraid to ask

Just in case I prove unworthy I work harder to
die
My productivity keeps getting called into
question
I don’t feel no ways tired

I wear my emotions on sweater sleeves
Empathy adorns me as deranged
Too bad it’s not high fashion

I bottled them cracked glasses cut hands
Lured heart’s sorrowful necessity for charity
To be returned here

HUNKER DOWN

"Fauci warns that the US needs to 'hunker
down" ahead of the coming flu season"
9/12/2020

They knelt on our necks/gunned
Us down in streets/strangled
Our hope/in chokeholds/until
There was no more/breath left
To breathe/they murdered/our
Daughters and sons/ransacked our
Neighborhoods/we be
Black/and took action/Hunkered
Down/in the streets/it was
Pre flu season/still/we
Found no safety.

They polluted air and land/
Still forcing us/to till the
Ground/we grew ill and weary/but
We knew/we had to eat/we be
Black/we fought to survive/Hunkered
Down/with necessary precautions/it was
Pre flu season/still/we were poisoned and dying.

She swallowed/warmth & moisture/picking

Up weight/and steam/until it became/
Nauseating/her regurgitation/was
Indiscriminate precipitation/heavings of
Winds/and waves/we be Black/
And fled the scene/we Hunkered
Down/in nearby communities/it was
Pre flu season/still/we found no relief.

They withheld resources/prayed
We'd self-destruct/as they
Gradually/moved in/renamed and
Staked claims/to our communities/
we be Black/and resisted/Hunkered
Down/and refused to move/it was
Pre flu season/still/we met bankruptcy.

They spoke of COVID-19/we
Were essential/and working/providing
For our families/we did/what was
Necessary/they ran rampantly/we be
Black/and cautious/we Hunkered
Down/in masks/well before/flu season
Still/there's no end within reach.

Fauci/has no more to offer/than
Another admonition/for Hunkering
Down/in our communities/but we be
Black/and been Hunkering Down/
With nothing else to do/and

Nothing/to show for it.

MONSTERS

Childs play waiting for mommies
To look away in the kitchen
Cooking on her feet tricking
To make the coins she hopes
Feeds the family another month
With a roof over all our heads

He waits for my loneliness
Lurking in the shadows
With anticipation hoping
To capitalize on the moment
To touch me when he knows
My screams will meet deaf ears
Or fall silent in chambers
Where they'll remain unheard

He degrades me in love's
Absence as I'm gazing
In the mirror and finding disdain
With no one else home
To offer a different perspective

Beauty is everything but me
All my contours fall just shy
Of perfection an asymmetric

Mess can't calculate
The standard deviation

I seek to marry the monster
Emerging from forced
Love for him
So he won't kill me

There are Monsters
In my closet.

FAMILY TIES

Knotted souls refuse to be disentangled
Obnoxiously bound and unrelenting
Deprecating articulations of judgment
Crown molding in the image of someone else
Installed in my heart as home
Alone in the crowded space
Where love only means control
And manipulation molds me as the problem

Firestarters burn the joy in my soul to ash
I inhale the smoke that tars the breath
I wished to purely breathe pollution
Trapped in the inescapable hell they call
holiness
Everything good invisible everything broken
including me
They say home is where the heart is
They are heartless warmth long turned cold
A wintry mix of emotion blended in
unforgiveness
Holding me hostage and blood trapped in
bondage

Lord prepare my way
Of escape

SANCTIFIED

Snatched out
From among them
Forced to be separate
Sanctified holy cast away
From things deemed unclean
Transformed by the infiltration
Of my mind indoctrination
Posing as renewal forsaking all
Following the path of self-
Righteousness casting stones
Claiming to be David but mostly Goliath
And giants come falling from pedestals
At the peak of staircases climbing
Towards heaven in pursuit of holiness
Still not receiving the promise
Silence where my praise used to be
Since burnt sacrifices left a stench
In God's nostrils with rejection inevitable
I was abominable by design
God defied their will with my creation
I was the one who came to earth
Destined for hell and the wails swell
In my sin stricken throat
Trapped where ears never hear
My side of the story

UNRAVELING

Like the string taut
In an effort to hide my fray
I found myself unraveling
Civility tearing at the seam
Respectability displaced
And the garments I made
No longer clothed me in praise

I scrambled to put the contents
Of my brokenness back
Into my shell hoping no one
Took notice of the mess I made
Or the depths in which I wallow
Where wading turns into drowning
In a twinkling of an eye

My hope now built on nothing
Less than the hope of salvation
Through cleansing blood and righteousness
I dare not trust the word of men
But lean on promises and Jesus's name
Whether Lord or ancestor to be
Determined but in search of something
That can deliver my soul

DRUNKEN LOVE

Disillusioned by denial
Dissociation by intoxication
Lured into fantastical escape
Where reality remains unaccounted for

Searching to fill voids with libation
Elixir used like anesthetics
Empty yearnings for more
Leave me unsatisfied

I turn up
The bottle until I
No longer see my
Reflection at the bottom

Until the pain in my chest
Is replaced with heartburn
Dark brown ointment numbing
The scent of fear with liquid courage

Running into the arms of the devil
To alleviate the pain of rejection
Curb the sting of abandonment
Repressing insecurity through avoidance

Chasing after acceptance I found
Affirmation slurred into love languages
Liquor blankets kept me warm
In the embrace of names
I can't ever remember

Mourning by morning begging for mercy
I wallow in guilt waiting
For shame to turn into covenant
Reconciliation would meet me at church
Surely forgiveness is what sin is made for

PENTECOSTAL MOTHERS

Pentecostal mothers smack the Black
off the backs of her children

Striking them with blows bleeding
their doors so evil passes over

She beats them into compliance
not sparing the rod neither spoiling the child

Her holy hands laying them prostrate
in prayer screaming supplications to God

She anoints their asses with oil
sweat pouring from her brow

It is in their DNA to sin like their fathers
but their evil won't dwell in her house

With force she makes them wail
cleansing them from wickedness

Damnation doesn't compare to the stripes
when they heal scars will welt in praise

While they direct their songs to heaven

she speaks in tongues clanking cymbals

Without love cracking whips of control
calling the space where her blows meet their
bodies

Psalms and lifts them to her God
her children weep in despair

Rebelling evermore willing
to take the beatings sure to come

Pretending to be tambourines making music
she sings at church on Sunday morning

REASONS USED TO JUSTIFY MY ABANDONMENT

Because I cut my hair
Because I had the audacity to put another hole in my ear
Because I had a boyfriend
Because I identified as queer
Because I was altogether unholy
Because my worship lacked sincerity
Because I was disobedient
Because I married a woman
Because I divorced her
Because I moved to a city I didn't call home
Because I didn't abandon my heart's desires
Because I didn't model my life in his fancy
Because I didn't meet his egotistical standards
Because I was unworthy of forgiveness
Because I deserved to be punished
Because I didn't do as he said
Because I chose myself
Because I didn't yield to his manipulation
Because he could not control me
Because I no longer benefit him
Because I was going to hell
So he might as well give me the preview

THE GIVER

The Lord giveth,
And the Lord taketh away.

Gave me two dead aunts
Just in time for my 8th birthday.
Took the normalcy out of life
Left me with missing pieces.

Gave me disruption that shook
My foundation cracked and crumbling
Took my support system
Left me without refuge to run to.

Gave me unrighteous tyrants
Shepherding my soul to submission
Took my confidence
Left me with doubt and ruptured innocence.

Gave me cycles of abandonment
Erratic irregularity replaced consistency
Took my faith doused in hope
Left me with perdition for paradise.

Gave me second chances
I never asked for
Took my success rate
Left me with unsought survival.

The Lord giveth,
And the Lord taketh away;
Ain't that why he's praised?

TURBULENT TRANSITIONS

Caught in metamorphosis
Betwixt indoctrination and intuition
My progress catches me in a conundrum.

Scriptures etched on my heart drip
Doctrine. Hermeneutics haunt me
With carceral exegesis:
Punishment and vengeance.
Ultimate judgment awaits.

Visions of me gnashing
My teeth in a cauldron
Of brimstone–burning
In hellfire and flames,
Crisply cast down from
Heaven. Falling crown
Without redemption.

Detoxing from religion
Meets conviction, battles
Fought in transition.
From bondage to freedom
Still caught in between them
And even if the grass isn't greener,
I still long to be on the other side.

AND I QUESTION...

And I question…
If love exists in reality
Or in the fissures of our hearts
Where life is partially fact mostly fiction
And we live in a paradise behind lies
That makes us believe
Things get better with time?

And I question…
If soul mates actually exist
Or if we spend our lives with the one
We can best put up with because
Happiness is a matter of tolerance
And true happiness doesn't really exist?

And I question…
If there is a designated path
Or if all paths lead to an ending
Is God there for guidance
Or simply overseeing
If I make a wrong turn
Is there still a happy ending
Within reach?

And I question
If this is the end or just the beginning?

LIKE BALANCE

I wanna feel like balance

Like too much of this
And too little of that
Came together and made
Something perfect

Like all of the not enoughs
And all the too muches
Collided and there I was

Incompetency and deficiency
Blended brilliantly making
Adequacy of flaws otherwise
Contributing to mediocrity

Overdone meets underwhelmed
And finds increased capacity
Recognizing polarizing extremes
Ain't never thrown a proper party

Extraneous and superfluous
Are toned down with the right dose
Of reasonability making magic
Of moderation and my existence is sufficient

Both/And infused instead
Of deconstructed a mixture
Composed of braided strands
Where blemishes don't paint the full picture

I wanna exist in stasis
Balanced between worlds
Liable to fall apart
Lacking foundation

Where the end of the day
Feels like working half as hard
As you've played and you live
To thrive another day

I wanna feel like balance

Like Too much of this
And too little of that
Came together and made
Something perfect

Like all the not enoughs
And all the too muches
Collided and there
I was like Balance

WHY NOT ME?

Didn't my Lord deliver
Daniel, Joseph, Job & David
Weren't they vindicated
Healed and rescued by thy hand?

Weren't multitudes fed
Salvaged and emancipated
In your presence?

So why not me?

Would You confine me
To this deserted land
With no promise of redemption
Circling deserts praying?

Hoping and wishing
You'd remove this cup from me
Neutralize the poison,
Sure to consume me
If you let it.

Can I possibly maintain
My nevertheless
Yield to your will

When mine is shortsighted
In comparison?

Can I keep it
Despite my shaken faith
Finding it hard
To believe in glory
That can exist
After this?

Will malfunctions
And dysfunctions
Manifest for my good?

Will you be faithful
And complete this
Alarmingly unfinished work
You began in me?

Can you help my unbelief?

Have you not said it
Shall you not preserve me
From my return to perdition
Reestablish my confidence
In endurance?

Can I remain steadfast
And unmovable

Never swallowed up
By affliction?

Is it possible?

Because if my Lord delivered
Daniel, Joseph, Job & David
Why wouldn't God deliver me?

GARDEN OF GETHSEMANE

I took the weight
I carried down
By the riverside

Troubles left
In the last moment
I can remember

Rest exists only
On the other side
Of letting go

I keep holding on

Whose yoke is this
Not easy or light
Still unlearning

Together unequally
Indebted to unbelief
Identifying as believer

Rest exists only
On the other side

Of letting go

I keep holding on

This cross I carry
To the hill on which
I eventually die

Alone to bear
With silent prayers
And seven last words

Rest will come when I let go
My God why hast thou forsaken me

MUSIC IN THE AIR

Conductors
Musicians and
Instruments
Create
Carefully
Crafted
Collaborations of
Distinct sounds
Melodic waves
Rain climaxes
Keeping our feet
Dancin' fingers
Snappin' heads
Boppin' churches
Bumpin' clubs
Jumping parties
Stay Lit

Consistency
Manifests
Moments
Born from
Rhythmic
Harmonies
Strategically

Placed in
Calculated
Measures
Speaking for
Spirits
Welcoming
Connection by
Way of
Eardrums
Chakras and
Physical radiations

Sounds
Satisfy
Broad
Audiences
Without
Compromise
Identity
Remains
Relevant
We please
God like
David
Every song
We write
We sing
Becomes
Tambourines

Jingling in the
Heart of
Worship
Heard in
Heaven
Angels rejoice
And we are glad

THE RAPTURE

Imagine trumpets sounding
Miles Dizzy Gillespie Armstong
Swiftly encroaching moments speeding
A twinkle in your eye

Gladys Bentley Marsha P Angelou rise
One by one Rustin Baldwin Ailey
Name by name Lorde Eckstein Jordan
Angels sing along in praise as you gaze
Upon the majesty of their procession

Introducing an impatiently waiting God
Swooping in to capture weary souls
And treasure children gone too long
Without redemption, you lift your eyes
Black queer fugitive abolitionists
Evaporating from the wiles of earth venturing
Into heaven feet dancing on golden streets
Adorned brides expecting beside crystalized rivers
Flowing along the throne of God marking the end
Old worlds won over by the newness born of revolution

Churches void of bigots in pulpits capitalists
Degenerating in sermons as their souls prepare
For eternal homes in flames beneath
While crucified bodies find their home in glory

Revolutionaries seated munching manna
Sipping grandeur made with milk and honey
Rejoicing as they enter the promised land

Corporations rot in hell turning to ash and dust
Can't accommodate the loss of servitude's
absence
The empire crumbles burying evil in the rubble
beneath

The collapse returning righteousness in
solidarity with believers
We've seen the last days of suffering and God
Came back as it was written

www.ingramcontent.com/pod-product-compliance
Lightning Source LLC
Chambersburg PA
CBHW062203160726
48282CB00027B/972
* 9 7 8 9 3 5 7 2 1 1 1 9 2 *